‘E DUE

Native American Foods and Recipes

Sharon Moore

The Rosen Publishing Group's

READING ROOM
Collection™

New York

The recipes in this cookbook are intended for a child to make together with an adult.

Published in 2002 by The Rosen Publishing Group, Inc.
29 East 21st Street, New York, NY 10010

First Library Edition 2002

Book Design: Ron A. Churley

Photo Credits: Cover, p. 1 © The Library of Congress/FPG International; p. 4 © Robert Holmes/Corbis; pp. 6, 22 © Photoworld/ FPG International; pp. 7, 15, 17 by Christine Innamorato and Olga Vega; p. 9 © Index Stock; p. 10 © National Archives/FPG International; pp. 14, 18, 20 © Corbis-Bettmann; p. 16 © Corbis.

Library of Congress Cataloging-in-Publication Data

Moore, Sharon, 1969-
  Native American foods and recipes / Sharon Moore.
     p. cm. — (The Rosen Publishing Group's reading room collection)
Includes index.
Summary: Discusses Native American cultures by focusing on their food and recipes.
  ISBN 0-8239-3727-5 (lib. bdg.)
  1. Indians of North America—Food—Juvenile literature. 2. Indian cookery—United States—Juvenile literature. [1. Indians of North America—Food. 2. Indian cookery. 3. Indians of North America—Social life and customs.] I. Title. II. Series.
  E98.F7 M66 2002
  394.1'089'97—dc21
                                        2001007014
Manufactured in the United States of America

For More Information
Native Peoples Magazine: Recipes
http://www.nativepeoples.com/np_features/np_recipes/recipes_main.html

Native American Culture
http://www.ewebtribe.com/NACulture/food.htm

Contents

Native American Food

Long ago, there were many Native American tribes in North America. Native Americans lived in five main areas of what is now known as the United States: the Southwest, the Pacific Coast, the Great Plains, the Northeast, and the South.

Each Native American tribe ate different kinds of food. Most Native Americans ate plants, berries, fruits, and vegetables. Some tribes grew their food on farms. Others gathered these foods from the land. Most Native Americans also hunted for meat. They ate the foods that were plentiful in the areas where they lived.

Native American tribes such as the Sioux hunted buffalo, which provided them with meat to eat and hides to wear to keep them warm.

The Southwest Indians

The Pueblo, Zuni, and Hopi Indians lived in hot, dry deserts in the southwestern part of the United States. They grew corn, beans, peppers, squash, and melons. They ground white corn to make **cornmeal** mush and used red and blue corn to make bread. The people of these tribes hunted rabbits and other animals. To get ready for winter, they stored foods such as corn and beans. They also collected the seeds of wild grasses and boiled the juice of cactus fruit to make **syrup** and jam.

The Pueblo Indians lived in homes made of stone or adobe. Adobe is made of clay or earth that is baked in the sun.

Indian Fry Bread

You will need:

2 cups flour
1 teaspoon baking
   powder
1/2 teaspoon salt
warm water
1/4 cup vegetable oil

How to do it:

Sift together flour,
baking powder, and
salt in a bowl. Slowly
add warm water while
stirring. Keep adding
water until you have
dough that feels like
mud. Mix and knead
dough until smooth. If
dough is sticky, sprinkle
with flour. Cover
dough with a towel
and let stand for 10
minutes. Break dough
into lemon-size pieces.
Roll each piece into a
ball and flatten into a
pancake. Heat oil in a
heavy frying pan. Add
as many pieces of
bread as will fit in the
pan. Fry on each side
until brown. Take
brown fry breads out
of oil with tongs and
place on a plate
covered with a paper
towel. Serve fry breads
with salt or maple
syrup. This recipe
serves about four
people.

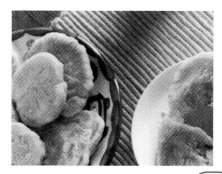

The Pacific Coast Indians

Native Americans in the Pacific Coast area had plenty of food to eat from the nearby forests and rivers. They gathered wild plants, berries, nuts, and **mushrooms** from the land. They also hunted wild animals in the forest.

The Pacific Coast tribes, such as the Kwakiutl (kwah-kee-OO-tuhl) and Sokomish, caught fish and cooked it over hot coals. They steamed **shellfish**, such as clams, on heated rocks. These tribes usually caught more fish than they could eat. They smoked the extra fish to keep it from spoiling and stored it so they would have it to eat during the winter.

Native Americans of the Pacific Coast relied on fish for much of their food. One traditional Native American way to fish is by using a spear.

The Great Plains Indians

Many Great Plains Indians, such as the Sioux, Blackfeet, and Crow, followed the buffalo that lived in this area. They hunted and ate buffalo meat and used the skins for clothing and **shelter**. When the Plains Indians were unable to find buffalo, they hunted deer and rabbits. They also gathered wild rice, seeds, and plants. Some tribes, such as the Mandan, did not move with the buffalo. Instead, they settled in one place and farmed the land. They grew corn, pumpkins, squash, and beans.

Snow Food

You will need:

1 tablespoon
    margarine or butter
1 cup maple syrup
1/2 teaspoon salt
1/2 cup pecans
8 cups popped
    popcorn
cooking spray

How to do it:

Lightly spray a large, shallow pan with cooking spray. Place popcorn and pecans in pan. In a medium saucepan, combine butter, syrup, and salt.

Cook over medium heat, stirring frequently, until mixture reaches 260°F on a candy thermometer. Pour hot syrup over popcorn and nuts. Mix gently to coat the popcorn. When mixture cools, break into pieces. Makes eight cups.

Native Americans of the Great Plains, like the Blackfeet, hunted buffalo. They used the buffalo for food and made teepee shelters out of buffalo hides.

The Northeast Indians

Many Native American tribes in the Northeast grew corn, beans, and squash. Tribes such as the Iroquois (EER-uh-kwoy) and Oneida (oh-NY-duh) planted these three crops together, which came to be known as the "three sisters." They believed that each crop was a special gift and would be protected by one of the three sister spirits. According to **legend**, the three sisters should never be apart from each other. They should be planted together, eaten together, and **celebrated** together.

Since they lived near water, the Northeast Indians always had fish and shellfish to eat. Some Native American tribes learned to **tap** the maple trees for sap and made maple syrup.

Native Americans in the Northeast were excellent farmers. They grew corn, beans, and squash, which they called the "three sisters."

Three Sisters

You will need:

1 small spaghetti
   squash
2 cups navy beans
1 cup cooked corn
1 red pepper, finely
   chopped
2 tablespoons butter
2 tablespoons olive oil
1/2 cup grated
   Parmesan cheese
2 tablespoons
   chopped parsley
2 tablespoons
   chopped basil

How to do it:

Preheat oven to 375°F.
Pierce squash with
knife. Wrap in foil. Bake
for 1 hour and 15
minutes. Remove and
cool. Combine beans
and corn. Heat in
small pan until hot.
Cut squash in half
lengthwise and
remove pasta-like
strands with fork. Place
in serving dish. Add
beans, corn, and
pepper and mix
together lightly. Melt
butter in small pan or
microwave. Stir in olive
oil and pour over
vegetables. Sprinkle
top with cheese,
parsley, and basil.
Makes eight servings.

Pumpkin-Corn Sauce

You will need:

1 15-ounce can plain
   pumpkin (without
   spices)
1 cup canned or
   frozen corn
1/2 teaspoon salt
2 tablespoons honey

How to do it:

Preheat oven to 350°F. Grease a baking sheet with a small amount of cooking oil. Place corn on the oiled baking sheet and bake for 20 minutes. Mix the corn, pumpkin, salt, and honey in a medium-size pot. Heat it over medium heat until it starts to bubble. Turn the heat to low and cook for 10 minutes, stirring from time to time. Serve with grilled chicken or pork. This recipe serves four people.

 Many Native Americans grew corn, squash, and pumpkins. You can use corn and pumpkins to make a tasty dish.

The Southern Indians

Native American tribes in the South grew corn, sweet potatoes, and peanuts. They also grew **hickory** nuts, which were boiled into a kind of milk used for cooking. Tribes such as the Cherokee, Seminole, and Creek made soups and breads using ground hickory nuts. Native Americans in this area ate meat and fish that they cooked into thick stews. The women made **pottery** bowls in which they served their food.

Today, some southern Native Americans, such as the Seminoles, eat a roasted corn soup called "sofkee."

Baked Sweet Potatoes

You will need:

4 medium-size sweet
    potatoes

How to do it:

Preheat oven to 400°F.
Scrub sweet potatoes
well under water. Poke
sweet potatoes several
times with a fork.
Cover a small baking
dish with foil. Put sweet
potatoes on foil and
put dish in the oven.
Bake for about one
hour. Take sweet
potatoes out of the
oven and slice open.
Serve with a bit of
butter, brown sugar, or
maple syrup on top.
Makes four servings.

Cooking and Baking

Most Native American tribes roasted their meat over an open fire. Southwestern and southern tribes baked meat and vegetables in clay pots that they buried in the ground with hot coals. Hours later, they dug up the pots, and the family meal was ready.

Some tribes cooked food in clay pots that had small holes in them. Steam flowed through the holes and cooked the food. Some tribes of the Southwest built clay ovens in which to bake corn bread and cook stews.

Some Native Americans still use clay ovens for baking breads and other foods.

Cranberry Corn Bread

You will need:

- 1 cup unbleached white flour
- 1-1/3 cups yellow cornmeal
- 1/2 teaspoon salt
- 1 tablespoon baking powder
- 1/2 cup cranberries
- 2 large eggs
- 1/4 cup honey
- 1 cup nonfat milk
- 2 tablespoons sunflower oil

How to do it:

Preheat oven to 400°F. Spray an 8-inch baking pan with cooking spray. In a bowl, mix flour, cornmeal, baking powder, and salt. Stir in cranberries. In another bowl, whisk together eggs, milk, honey, and oil. Add dry ingredients and mix until blended. Pour batter into pan. Bake until top is lightly browned and a toothpick inserted in the middle comes out clean, about 30 minutes.

Food for Traveling

While they were at home, most Native Americans ate one big meal a day. Native American men often had to travel away from home for many days at a time to hunt or fish. For these trips, the women made special foods for the men to take with them. These foods were easy to carry, tasted good, and did not spoil. They also kept the men strong and healthy during their journey.

When they traveled, Native Americans brought special foods that could be carried easily. These foods included dried meats, berries, and turnips.

The women made dried meat cakes or Indian jerky, which was also made of dried meat. These foods were eaten as the main meal on the road. Some Native Americans carried a mixture of fine corn flour and sweet syrup to eat with the meat. Others carried a mixture of dried berries and turnips.

Indian Ice Cream

You will need:

1 quart fresh berries (raspberries, strawberries, blueberries, or blackberries)
1/2 cup honey

How to do it:

Blend berries and honey in a blender. Chill this mixture and serve. This recipe makes about four to six servings.

Native Americans mixed dried berries, fish oil, and snow to make this tasty treat.

Sharing Food

Native Americans farmed, hunted, fished, and gathered food from forests. They ate different kinds of food that they found on the land where they lived. Native Americans shared the belief that food was a special gift from Earth. They did not waste any of it, and they never ate alone. Sharing food with family was a very important part of their celebrations, and a time to give thanks. Preparing, eating, and sharing special foods is still an important part of family celebrations for Native Americans today.

Food continues to be an important part of Native American life. Families share in preparing and eating special foods during their celebrations.

Glossary

celebrate   To do something special in honor of a special person or day.

cornmeal   Ground, dried corn used to make breads and other foods.

hickory   A North American tree with nuts that can be eaten.

legend   A story from the past that many people believe.

mushroom   A small vegetable shaped like an umbrella.

pottery   Pots, dishes, or vases made from clay and baked until they are hard.

shellfish   A water animal with a hard shell, such as an oyster or a clam.

shelter   Something that covers or protects you from the weather.

syrup   A sweet, thick liquid.

tap   To make a hole in a tree to let sap flow out.

Index